DOGS

A GUIDE FOR HEALTH, HYGIENE, AND HAPPINESS

CÉLINE GASTINEL-MOUSSOUR

Translation by Zachary R. Townsend

WORKMAN PUBLISHING · NEW YORK

The content of this book is for informational purposes only and is not intended to diagnose or prevent any condition or disease. Consult your veterinarian before changing pet care.

Library of Congress Cataloging-in-Publication Data is available.
ISBN 978-1-5235-2309-2

Design by Lisa Hollander

Photo Credits: Front Cover: cynoclub/Shutterstock.com (dog), Julieanne Browning (ingredients) **Back Cover:** Napat (dog), Julieanne Browning (ingredients). **Front Matter:** Scisetti Alfio/Shutterstock.com (herb), dezy Shutterstock.com (dog) **Table of Contents:** Gladskikh Tatiana/Shutterstock.com **Sandra Mahut:** pp. 5, 16, 37, 41, 43, 44, 48, 61, 65, 78. **Émilie Provost Photographie:** p. 84. **Shutterstock.com**: Ermolaev Alexander: pp. 40, 46. Scisetti Alfio: p. 57. artphotoclub: p. 33. COLOA Studio: p. 53. Cynoclub: p. 58. domnitsky: p. 81. fotohunter: pp. 82–83. GoodFocused: pp. 18, 35, 36, 39, 72, 74. Liudmyla Guniavaia: p. 38. Happy Monkey: p. 12. Jiang Hongyan: p. 31. Eric Isselee: pp. 6, 30. Ludmila Ivashchenko: p. 25. Ammit Jack: p. viii. Jagodka: p. 15. jajam_e: p. 75. JR foto: p. 23. Patryk Kosmider: p. 8. Kotkoa: pp. vi–vii. Erik Lam: pp. 20, 32. Life in Pixels: p. 68. Dorottya Mathe: p. 2. Dorota Milej: p. 51. MirasWonderland: p. 80. MRAORAOR: p. 79. Napat: p. 11. New Africa: p. 73. Malikova Oksana: p. 69. Otsphoto: p. 22. outc: p. 54. RazoomGame: p. 62. Reshetnikov_art: p. 26. Elena Schweitzer p. 63. Sevenke: p. 76. Tanya Sid: p. 64. Snezhana_G: p. 59. Barna Tanko: p. 67. tsik: p. 1. Jne Valokuvaus: p. 29.

Workman books are available at special discounts when purchased in bulk for premiums and sales promotions as well as for fundraising or educational use. Special editions or book excerpts can also be created to specification. For details, please contact special.markets@hbgusa.com.

Workman Publishing Co., Inc., a subsidiary of Hachette Book Group, Inc.
1290 Avenue of the Americas
New York, NY 10104

workman.com

WORKMAN is a registered trademark of Workman Publishing Co., Inc.,
a subsidiary of Hachette Book Group, Inc.

Printed in China on responsibly sourced paper.
First printing June 2023
10 9 8 7 6 5 4 3 2 1

WELLNESS for
DOGS

Contents

Introduction

As dog owners, we have many types of solutions to consider for supporting the health and well-being of our canine companions. We strive each day to offer our pets their best and most comfortable lives. Natural plant-based remedies can be an important ally in this endeavor. Through their wide variety of health benefits, plants provide overall body support and relief while also acting as a complement to conventional treatments during more critical health conditions.

Because each dog reacts differently to medicines, food, natural care, and even their relationships with their human companions, plants allow us to tailor recipes and preparations to individualize our pets' needs. Who better to observe these differences and offer a dog a unique, tailor-made natural solution than its owner?

In this book, you will find simple recipes whose benefits have been proven through years of use. These recipes are the fruits of my daily work as a veterinarian, but they also reflect knowledge and experience passed down from generations. When trying a new treatment, always start with a low dose and keep a close eye on your dog for reactions.

My canine patients are the ones who teach me the most about the effectiveness of a plant's health benefits. Seeing their positive responses inspires my work more and more each day.

*A hydrosol, also known as floral water, is a distillation of water and plant material. You can buy them ready made or make them yourself. Always be sure anything you buy is therapeutic grade.

*In all places that recommend a "capsule" of natural product (e. g. rhodiola rosea), consult the dosing directions on the container for animal weight.

PRECAUTIONS

- Clean and dry all utensils using a clean cloth.

- Clean and sanitize the work surface.

- Wash and dry your hands using a clean cloth reserved just for this task.

- Properly store all ingredients and finished preparations.

- Always be sure to use **therapeutic grade** essential oils.

CHAPTER 1

Hygiene, Daily Life, and Mental Well-Being

For a Beautiful Coat

The condition of a dog's coat reflects its health and well-being. Under normal circumstances, there is no need to bathe our dogs often—once a month is sufficient. However, when our furry friends become muddy or smelly, it's always useful to have a good-quality lightly scented homemade natural shampoo on hand. If your dog needs cleaning in only a small area, a quick alternative to a bath is to use a puppy washing mitt or soft cloth with just a little all-natural soap, such as savon de Marseille (Marseille soap), to wash the affected area. Always rinse the coat thoroughly and dry with a towel.

What to Know

If the temperature of the room is cold, it is important to thoroughly dry your dog's coat after each washing. If using an electric dryer, set it to the coolest setting. You can also create a warm room by increasing the heat in the washroom while staying close to your dog until its coat is dry. This also gives you the opportunity to brush the coat while it's drying.

Natural Solutions

▶ Aloe vera gel: moisturizing, soothing, and healing.

▶ Hydrosols with trace amounts of essential oil compounds have a lighter scent to prevent overwhelming a dog's sensitive sense of smell.

▶ Lavender hydrosol: soothing and healing.

▶ Rose hydrosol: healing.

▶ Calendula hydrosol: for delicate or irritated skin.

▶ Verbena hydrosol: soothing with a mild scent.

Natural Shampoo

WELLNESS RECIPE for DOGS

2 tablespoons neutral glycerin cleansing base

1 tablespoon hydrosol of your choice

1 teaspoon aloe vera gel (optional)

1. In a small bowl, combine all the ingredients.

2. Use a puppy washing mitt or soft cloth to gently clean the dirty area.

Variation: The addition of aloe vera gel is optional; it makes this shampoo ideal for dry or sensitive skin.

Tip: Preparing only the amount needed each time will prevent the need to store the shampoo, since it is used only about once per month.

WHY A NEUTRAL PH?

A dog's skin has a pH of 7. Using a cleansing base with a neutral pH (pH = 7) allows the shampoo to be effective without being too harsh. A glycerin base helps keep the skin well hydrated.

Seasonal Shedding

Both short-haired and long-haired dogs shed on a regular basis although more noticeably in spring and autumn during normal seasonal shedding periods. In recent years, however, shedding seems to occur throughout the year and on a more constant basis, possibly caused by environmental factors as well as increasingly urban lifestyles in which dogs spend little time outdoors.

What to Know

There is no miracle solution to limit shedding, but it is possible to promote regrowth and a beautiful shiny coat. A controlled indoor temperature that is not too hot, regular brushings that massage the skin and promote good overall health, and long walks outdoors that offer a dog an environment as close to a natural lifestyle as possible are all positive factors that help address the quality and regularity of shedding. Poodles, specifically, do not shed (or are low shedding) and thus need regular shearing and frequent brushing.

Natural Solutions

▶ Spirulina has antioxidant and positive effects on the liver and digestion.

▶ Probiotics help with the absorption of nutrients and the health of gut flora.

▶ Brewer's yeast provides vitamins, minerals, and amino acids beneficial to dander, and dogs often enjoy it. (It's a good feeling to provide our dogs with a treat they enjoy while also boosting the health of their gut flora.)

▶ Inulin, a prebiotic, is contained in dandelion root and has a positive effect.

Brewer's Yeast *and* Spirulina

WELLNESS **RECIPE** *for DOGS*

Equal doses are needed for Brewer's yeast and spirulina tablets.

BREWER'S YEAST and SPIRULINA TABLETS
dosed at 500mg per tablet

WEIGHT	DOSE
2-11 pounds (1-5 kg)	¼ tablet each
12-22 pounds (5-10 kg)	½ tablet each
23-44 pounds (10-20 kg)	1 tablet each
44-110 pounds (20-50 kg)	2 tablets each
110-130 pounds (50-60 kg)	2½ tablets each
Over 130 pounds (60 kg)	3 tablets each

Tip: For sensitive dogs, start at a quarter of the dose and gradually increase the dosage. This provides time for a dog to adjust and develop a tolerance. Use no more than one full dose a day during shedding season.

A MATTER OF MICROBIOTA

The beauty of a dog's coat is directly related to its overall good health, the quality of its digestion, and, specifically, the good health of its gut microbiota. Brewer's yeast and spirulina promote healthy gut flora!

The Eyes

Dogs' eyes, eyelids, and the entire area around the eyes are very sensitive and should receive regular and very gentle cleansing. Natural solutions best for this task can be difficult to come by, but they do exist, such as those containing a hyaluronic acid and aloe vera gel, which help the eyes maintain a healthy level of hydration.

What to Know

Because dogs have very delicate and sensitive eyes, it is always important to clean them after a walk through a dusty environment; in cold, dry, and windy weather; or after contact with grasses and leaves or sand and seawater. Physiological saline in single dosing vials is an excellent option, but it is possible to make your own solution.

Natural Solutions

▶ Chamomile and cornflower are two hydrosols effective for cleaning the eyes.

▶ Roman chamomile can also be used when prepared as a tisane— or a warm tea. Caution: Always allow the tisane to cool first before using it!

STRICT RULES OF HYGIENE

When preparing any homemade solution for cleaning your dog's eyes, it is imperative to observe very strict rules of hygiene—worthy of those followed in a pharmaceutical laboratory! The goal is to clean and soften the eyes, not to introduce additional bacteria into them.

It is best to prepare only the amount of solution needed for a single application to avoid problems with storing excess. Whenever possible, use bottles or jars that have never been used.

WELLNESS RECIPE for DOGS

Chamomile Tisane *for the* Eyes

3 tablespoons + 1 teaspoon (50 ml) water

2 teaspoons dried Roman chamomile flowers

1. Bring the water to a boil and pour it over the chamomile flowers. Cover, and let infuse for 5 minutes.

2. Strain it and let it cool.

3. Apply to the eyes with a compress. You can also use a sterile compress, if desired.

Variation: After letting the chamomile tisane cool, add 1 tablespoon of cornflower hydrosol.

Tip: There is no miracle solution for the tear stains around the eyes, where the hairs are stained pink by the pigmented secretions from the eyes, but regular cleaning with a chamomile tisane is a good habit.

The Ears

Although most dogs experience no problems with their ears throughout their lives, some may experience inflammation or bacterial or fungal infections. This occurs more often in dogs with drooping ears. Because of their delicate nature, the ears should be proactively monitored rather than regularly cleaned. If the ears are not experiencing a problem, generally there is no need to clean them. Consult a veterinarian when any serious problems are observed.

What to Know

Maintaining healthy flora in a dog's ears is important for avoiding infections and maintaining good health.

Several other factors can inversely impact a dog's ear health, such as diet, contact allergies that may occur when a dog rolls on carpets made of synthetic materials, exposure to dust and dirt from renovations in the home, or exposure to everyday cleaning products.

For good ear health, it is also vital to avoid exposure to the cold such as a cold bath or cold draft (an air conditioner or fan that is too close, for example).

THREE EAR CLEANING SCENARIOS

When it becomes necessary to clean your dog's ears, always be gentle.

• If the ears just need maintenance: Cleaning with aloe vera gel is a perfect choice in this situation. You can also add a lavender or calendula hydrosol.

• If your dog has mild inflammation: Before consulting a veterinarian, clean the ears with the ear cleansing recipe below.

• If your dog has an ear infection and is being treated with conventional solutions: Use the cleansing recipe on page 81 before administering the treatment.

Gentle Ear Cleanser

1 tablespoon stabilized aloe vera gel

1 tablespoon calendula or lavender hydrosol

1. Thoroughly combine the ingredients.

2. Apply gently with a clean cloth around the ears. Never go inside the ears. If you are concerned about inner ear issues, consult your veterinarian.

3. Store the cleanser in a small bottle in the refrigerator for up to 10 days.

Tip: Ideally, just as when treating the eyes, it is best to prepare only the amount of cleanser needed for one application. However, there is one tip that will allow you to store the solution for several weeks: Prepare the cleanser with an aloe vera gel from an unused bottle, then freeze the cleanser in an ice cube tray. Thaw only the quantity needed. Another tip is to use a stabilized orally safe aloe vera gel made for animals.

The Mouth

A dog's mouth plays many important roles. In addition to its common functions, a dog's mouth acts as our hands do, allowing the animal to catch objects, such as toys. Dogs also use their mouths to wash and maintain their coats. The dog's mouth is host to many beneficial bacteria but also to others that can produce odors and cause tartar buildup that can lead to infections and loosening of the teeth.

FIGHTING INFLAMMATION

If we were to be diligent about brushing our dogs' teeth each day, problems with mouth odor, gum inflammation, and tartar buildup would be rare. But experience proves that, as dog owners, we tend to not be very diligent with this task. Dogs often seem to have an unpleasant-smelling mouth. One natural ingredient particularly effective against inflammation and bacteria is lactoferrin. However, it is expensive and does not mix well with other ingredients—all the more reason to use the following solution.

What to Know

When the environment within a dog's mouth is out of balance, the gums become red, inflamed, and painful—and the smell can be very unpleasant. For prevention, the physical act of brushing the dog's teeth has the most positive results; using a natural solution when performing this task introduces good hygiene and a pleasant smell.

Natural Solutions

▶ When considering both preventive and curative tooth

care solutions, avoid giving your dog bones to gnaw to "clean" the teeth, as the conventional wisdom goes. The risk of intestinal obstruction is high if the dog ingests pieces of bone.

▶ Choose simple solutions such as a mouth cleanser for prevention, possibly with the addition of propolis when mouth odor is a bit strong.

Mouth Cleanser

WELLNESS
RECIPE
for DOGS

3 tablespoons + 1 teaspoon (50 ml) water

1 tablespoon dried lemon balm leaves

1 tablespoon lemon hydrosol

1 tablespoon stabilized aloe vera gel

1. Bring the water to a boil and pour it over the leaves. Cover, and let infuse for 5 minutes.

2. Add the hydrosol and the aloe vera gel.

3. Strain it and let it cool.

4. Gently apply the cleanser to your dog's teeth using a soft toothbrush or a cotton finger brush (available online).

Variation: Add a capsule of propolis powder.

The Paw Pads

A dog's paw pads are one of its most fascinating features. They are just as unique as our own fingerprints. The role of the paw pads is to cushion and provide support on the ground, to make a dog's movements silent, and to help avoid injuries. Paradoxically, the thick and rigid skin of the paw pads can often be a source of injuries. They can crack in cold weather or overheat when the dog walks on either very hot ground such as sand or asphalt or over very cold surfaces such as snow or ice.

What to Know

Applying a small amount of a mixture of essential oils to the paw pads will help discourage a dog from licking them due to minor injuries. Add aloe vera gel to soften the thick skin and prevent cracking.

Natural Solutions

▶ For cleaning, you can use the Thyme and Rosemary Tisane recipe on page 41.

ORAL SOLUTIONS

When dogs return home from time outdoors, a good habit is to clean and moisturize their paw pads, but, naturally, they will most often lick any solution you have carefully applied. For this reason, use ingestible solutions such as orally safe aloe vera gel, which has benefits not only when applied locally but also when ingested.

▶ A lavender or rose hydrosol is very suitable.

▶ The essential oils in the Healing Solution for Paw Pads (below) are soothing and healing.

WELLNESS RECIPE for DOGS

Healing Solution *for* Paw Pads

1 drop therapeutic grade lavender essential oil (*Lavandula angustifolia*)

1 drop Bourbon geranium essential oil

10 drops olive oil

20 drops Solubol (an all-natural emulsifier)

1 tablespoon boiled water or mineral water

1. Combine all the ingredients.

2. After drying the paw pads, apply about 4 drops to ⅛ teaspoon (0.2 to 0.5 ml) of the solution to the paw pads 1 to 4 times a day with a clean, soft cloth.

Variation: You can add 1 teaspoon of orally safe aloe vera gel to this mixture.

Tips:

▶ Because Solubol is stabilized, you can prepare a bottle of this solution and keep it in the refrigerator for up to 2 weeks.

▶ When a paw pad is cut or nicked, it is a good idea to put a bootie on the dog during its walk to prevent the wound from opening up with each step.

Localized Irritation

Natural preparations are perfectly suited as a first line of treatment for localized irritations, such as a small area of irritated skin that the dog licks or scratches or a recurring trivial injury.

What to Know

Honey is effective for healing wounds, but it is best to apply it under a bandage, as it can be quickly licked away. One tip is to add a small amount of diluted essential oil that will not only help with healing and disinfecting but will also act as a deterrent to the dog's nose and tongue.

Natural Solutions

▶ Apply a soothing, healing, moisturizing, and rejuvenating homemade solution (see page 15) morning and evening to any irritated areas.

▶ Other natural solutions are also suitable, such as aloe vera gel, essential oil solutions prepared as appropriately diluted sprays—which discourage licking and help with healing—and lavender hydrosol.

HELP DISCOURAGE LICKING

The legs are a common source of irritation after outdoor activities, such as a walk through tall grasses or wooded areas, for example. After returning home, consider slipping a special protective sleeve, some types of which can be attached around the dog's chest for the front legs or the hindquarters for the back legs, over the irritated leg to prevent the habit of biting and licking, which could cause minor wounds to heal slowly and become more painful.

Solution *for* Minor Irritation

WELLNESS
RECIPE
for DOGS

3 tablespoons + 1 teaspoon (50 ml) water

1 tablespoon dried thyme leaves

1 tablespoon dried mallow flowers

About ¼ teaspoon colloidal oats

1 tablespoon stabilized aloe vera gel

1. Bring the water to a boil and pour it over the leaves and flowers. Cover, and let infuse for 5 minutes.

2. Strain it and let it cool.

3. Add the oats and the aloe vera gel. Stir to combine.

4. Clean the irritated area with the solution 1 to 4 times a day. This solution is both cleansing and soothing. It can be prepared a few days ahead and stored in the refrigerator.

Tip: You can freeze the solution in ice cube trays and thaw small portions as you need them. It will keep in this way for a maximum of 1 month.

Intimate Hygiene

Cleaning around your dog's intimate areas (vulva, prepuce, anus) is a topic not often discussed, but it is nonetheless very important. Dogs wash themselves in these areas by licking, so it is very important to clean and dry these areas when they are soiled.

What to Know

The risk of soiling intimate areas is especially high in cases of diarrhea, and this can increase the risk of a urinary tract infection in female dogs if the area around the anus remains unclean. When the hair is long, a good trimming will make these areas easier to clean.

Natural Solutions

▶ Thyme has disinfectant and anti-inflammatory properties. Basil (*Ocimum basilicum*) adds to the antimicrobial effect, as it protects mucous membranes and acts as a decongestant.

▶ Adding lavender or calendula hydrosol makes the solution milder and more healing. After cleansing, apply orally safe aloe vera gel to help with healing and limit irritation and discomfort.

THE POWERS OF MARSEILLE SOAP

For simple and effective hygiene in these areas, rub a piece of all-natural savon de Marseille (Marseille soap) on a puppy washing mitt or soft cloth. Gently clean the soiled area. Rinse thoroughly and dry.

Intimate Hygiene Solution

3 tablespoons + 1 teaspoon (50 ml) water

1 tablespoon dried thyme leaves

1 tablespoon dried basil leaves

1 teaspoon lavender or calendula hydrosol

1. Bring the water to a boil and pour it over the leaves. Cover, and let infuse for 5 minutes.

2. Strain it and let it cool. Add the hydrosol.

3. Apply gently with a clean cloth to the area of concern.

Tip: The solution can be kept for 1 day in the refrigerator. This recipe can be used for both cleaning and treating.

External Parasites

There are many external parasites that can affect your canine friend, including ear mites, fleas, mosquitoes, and ticks. Treating and repelling these parasites with natural solutions is a complex topic because plants that kill and repel external parasites can often also be toxic to dogs.

What to Know

Many plants have antiparasitic properties, but this poses a problem: For a product to kill parasites, it must be toxic, which can present a real danger to the dog being treated. Dog owners should rely only on natural solutions that have been proven through long-term use to be both effective and safe, especially for those used to treat fleas.

PREVENTION

In areas where serious or even fatal diseases are carried by external parasites, conventional products for treating parasites are essential. When using traditional treatments, remember to protect your dog's liver and body as a whole. One of the most effective ways to do this is with phycocyanin, a blue-colored protein pigment found in spirulina.

Natural Solutions

▶ Food grade Diatomaceous earth is very popular for treating external parasites. It is a powder and should not be inhaled. It is typically combined with a vegetable oil to prevent this. Its effectiveness in destroying parasites is due to the formation of small shards of minerals that pierce an insect's outer coating, causing the parasite to dehydrate and die. These shards are immediately destroyed if they come in contact with water, however. A dog's hair will be sticky once it's mixed with oil and applied, but it can be applied before a walk outdoors in dry weather. Afterward, a good shampoo helps to eliminate the oil while the skin remains well hydrated.

▶ Neem oil is also popular, and a tisane using neem and walnut leaves (see below) is an effective preparation. Apply the tisane to the coat once a week as a preventative measure.

Preventive Parasite Spray

WELLNESS RECIPE for DOGS

Scant ½ cup (100 ml) water

1 tablespoon neem leaves

1 tablespoon walnut leaves

2 teaspoons lavender hydrosol

1. Bring the water to a boil and pour it over the leaves. Cover, and let infuse for 5 minutes.

2. Strain it and let it cool.

3. Add the hydrosol to provide a light and pleasant scent to the coat.

4. Apply to your dog's coat.

Internal Parasites

Throughout their lives, dogs risk contracting worms from sources such as contaminated soil, infected prey, or external parasites, to name a few. Worms that invade a dog's intestines can lead to very serious diarrhea. Other parasites can become lodged in the heart or lungs, so controlling worms—and taking preventive measures—is vital.

What to Know

A well-functioning gut offers powerful immunity and allows a dog to better eliminate internal parasites naturally. Offering probiotics and prebiotics is therefore a great option to achieve this. Consider treatment for worms at least three times a year, especially in spring and autumn.

Natural Solutions

▶ Pumpkin seeds are traditionally used to control taenia (tapeworms) and anise seeds to control roundworms.

In the recipe below, we add a little olive oil to bind the ground seeds into a paste to make it easier to administer. In general, dogs enjoy the taste of olive oil.

Deworming Seed Paste

1 fresh pumpkin seed per 11 pounds (5 kg) of body weight

1 anise seed per 11 pounds (5 kg) of body weight

Several drops olive oil

1. Thoroughly crush the seeds using a mortar and pestle.

2. Incorporate the olive oil to make a paste.

3. Mix with your dog's meal. Consult your veterinarian for how many doses your dog needs.

CHAPTER 2

Behavior and Activity

Remaining Calm in Uncertain Circumstances

Different types of dogs can respond differently to the same set of circumstances, depending on their temperament. Some seem to adapt to change pretty easily and some really do not. Generally, most dogs love routine and familiar places and fear change. Older dogs often have trouble with traveling during family vacations, with visits to the vet or groomer, as well as with strangers in the home. Soothing plants can offer great comfort during these times (see also Anti-Stress Tisane, page 27).

What to Know

A dog's ultrasensitive nose is one of its best assets. We have experienced how a smell can transport us back to a happy moment—or a stressful one—so imagine how a dog responds, with

---

A REASSURING SCENT

You can create calming surroundings for your dog by taking the security of the home with you through familiar smells. For example, is there a particular spice you use in a homemade baked good whose aroma and flavor your dog loves? If so, you can bake a batch of these treats with the associated smell and take them with you on trips.

a sense of smell that is thirty-five times more sensitive than our own! A dog maps out its world through its nose.

Natural Solutions

▶ Calming essential oils: petitgrain bigarade, neroli (from bitter orange), sweet orange, bergamot, fragrant verbena, ylang-ylang, and vanilla.

▶ For motion sickness: lavender essential oil.

Calming Room Spray

WELLNESS
RECIPE
for DOGS

2 teaspoons (10 ml) water

40 drops Solubol (an all-natural emulsifier)

5 drops lavender essential oil

1. Combine all the ingredients.

2. Fill a small spray bottle and shake it lightly.

3. Spray the mixture in the air near your dog. Never spray at the dog or in its face.

Tip: To determine if your dog likes the smell, spray it from a distance and see how your dog sniffs the air and approaches it. Sweet orange essential oil can be added to mellow out the aroma of lavender essential oil.

Before a trip, start using this spray around the home so your dog will associate it with home. Another option is to use it for the dog's crate or bed.

Stress

Stress for a dog can manifest itself in different ways. Some dogs develop extreme attachment to their owners or other familiar animals in the house and can become agitated in the absence of these companions. In others, the slightest disruption in routine or changes to familiar places becomes a source of anxiety and restlessness. This makes it nearly impossible for some pet owners to leave their dogs alone or to make any significant changes to their surroundings. Just as with humans, dogs can develop chronic health conditions when they experience too much stress.

What to Know

It is important to support the emotional well-being of your pet. There are several plants and herbs that can help soothe a dog's anxiety, including valerian. (Valerian is best used in a preparation along with other herbs to mask its unpleasant smell.)

Natural Solutions

▶ One of the most effective preparations to fight stress in dogs is a mixture of passionflower, valerian, and lemon balm.

▶ In the recipe below, a combination of linden flowers and orange blossom water makes a tisane that some dogs love. In addition to reducing stress, this tisane offers the spasmolytic effect of lemon balm and linden, which limit intestinal discomfort and diarrhea.

SERVING A LIQUID

To make a liquid preparation or tisane easier to consume, try dipping your pet's favorite treat or dry food into the liquid.

Anti-Stress Tisane

WELLNESS
RECIPE
for DOGS

3 tablespoons + 1 teaspoon (50 ml) water

1 tablespoon dried lemon balm leaves

1 tablespoon dried linden flowers

1 tablespoon orange blossom water

1. Bring the water to a boil and pour it over the leaves and flowers. Cover, and let it infuse for 5 minutes.

2. Strain it and let it cool.

3. Add the orange blossom water.

4. Administer 1 teaspoon (5 ml) per 22 pounds (10 kg) of body weight 1 to 3 times a day.

Tip: Start administering natural soothing solutions before any big event that may be stressful for your canine companion. For vacation travel, it's a good idea to offer the preparation a few days before departure, continue while on your trip, and then stop once you've returned home.

Adapting

Assisting with adapting to physical and environmental stressors is another often overlooked area in which plant-based preparations can be of benefit to your dog. Adaptogens are limited in number, but they can be very useful when offered.

What to Know

It is best to administer an adaptogen in the morning and, for dogs who tend to wake in the middle of the night, a calming solution in the evening. Consider using the Calming Room Spray (page 25) and the Anti-Stress Tisane (page 27) together and associate them, according to your dog's temperament, with shared pleasant outdoor activities or positive social situations.

Natural Solutions

▶ Ginseng is widely used to assist with helping the body adapt to change.

▶ Rhodiola rosea, also known as arctic root or golden root,

WHEN TO USE AN ADAPTOGEN

• in young dogs that have difficulty adjusting to their new families

• in dogs that experience motion sickness

• in dogs that engage in physical activities or competitions

• in cases of change such as a new home, new family, sadness, or separation

• in older dogs with diminished ability to adapt to changes

grows in cold climates. It is used to prevent fatigue and help with low energy. In older dogs, it offers support for low mental performance and lack of energy but without disrupting sleep. It also improves resistance to stress and fights depression.

Adaptogen

1 capsule rhodiola rosea for a dog weighing 22 to 44 pounds (10 to 20 kg)

1 capsule ginger for a dog weighing 22 to 44 pounds (10 to 20 kg)

Give your dog 1 capsule of each (less for smaller dogs) every morning.

Tips:
▶ Both are beneficial for dogs, but speak to your veterinarian if you have concerns about using them every day.

▶ As well as acting as an adaptogen, ginger is effective for dogs that lack an appetite. For that purpose, mash a small slice of fresh ginger using a mortar and pestle. Administer 1 drop of the juice per 11 pounds (5 kg) of body weight, with a maximum of 4 drops.

Mental Function

Dogs are living longer, so it is important to help ensure that their aging brains continue to function properly. An aging brain can lead to a dog's confusion about its surroundings, which can be distressing for the entire family.

What to Know

Spirulina, or more precisely phycocyanin, the blue-colored protein pigment contained in spirulina, has been shown to benefit brain function.

A dog's age at which owners should begin thinking about brain function depends on many factors, especially the breed. Generally speaking, the larger and heavier the dog, the more quickly it ages. Administering a spirulina-based food supplement can begin starting from age five for the large Bernese mountain dog, for instance, and age seven in a Chihuahua or Yorkshire terrier. The red pigment in fruits such as mulberries and blackberries (anthocyanins) contains antioxidants that benefit the brain cells for both humans and dogs. Some

IN CASE OF SURGERY

Stop administering ginkgo biloba to your dog four days prior to any surgical procedure as a precautionary measure because of its potentially blood-thinning effect.

red berries are unhealthy for dogs, so proceed with caution.

Natural Solutions

▶ Ginkgo biloba is particularly recommended in cases of decreased brain function. Its protective effects on nerve cells, blood vessels, and the brain's use of glucose—the fuel for brain cells—improves cognitive function, which in simpler terms means the brain's ability to perceive, reason, adapt, and interact. Ginkgo biloba is available in several forms. For dogs, alcohol-free extracts are recommended.

Ginkgo Leaf Tisane

WELLNESS RECIPE for DOGS

1 tablespoon + 1 teaspoon (20 ml) water

1 tablespoon dried ginkgo biloba leaves

1. Bring the water to a boil and pour it over the leaves. Cover, and let infuse for 5 minutes.

2. Strain it and let it cool.

3. Each morning, administer about ⅛ to ¼ teaspoon (0.5 to 1 ml) of tisane per 2¼ pounds (1 kg) of body weight (or about ½ teaspoon to a full teaspoon for every 10 pounds).

Sleep Schedule

There are two phases in a dog's life when you may need to focus on setting a sleep schedule: around the age of two months, when a weaned puppy arrives home with its new family, and at an advanced age when a dog may be losing cognitive function and forget that nighttime is for sleeping.

Natural Solutions

▶ For young dogs, a mixture of lemon balm, passionflower, and valerian can be calming and promote longer periods of sleep. Puppies tend to awaken at the end of each sleep cycle, which can be particularly bothersome.

▶ For older dogs, linden hydrosols and orange blossom water can provide relief for families when the dog has difficulty falling asleep or wakes in the middle of the night and begins vocalizing. The recommended dose is about 2 drops (0.1 ml) per 2¼ pounds (1 kg) of body weight. If the dog is also stressed or restless, a mixture of lemon balm, passionflower, and valerian can be effective. For melatonin, the recommended dose is 1 mg for a dog weighing 22 to 44 pounds (10 to 20 kg) and less for smaller dogs. If the dog tends to toss and turn day and night, Adaptogen Capsules (page 29) administered in the morning can be a helpful treatment. During the day, expose the dog to as much daylight as possible, and in the evening, create dark and calming surroundings.

Sleep-Promoting Tisane

WELLNESS RECIPE for DOGS

Scant ½ cup (100 ml) water

2 tablespoons dried lemon balm leaves

2 tablespoons dried linden flowers

1 tablespoon orange blossom buds

1. Bring the water to a boil and pour it over the leaves, flowers, and buds. Cover, and let infuse for 5 minutes.

2. Strain it and let it cool.

3. Each evening, administer about ⅛ teaspoon (0.5 ml) per 2¼ pounds (1 kg) of body weight, or about a teaspoon per 18 pounds. Note that linden is a diuretic, so your dog may need a trip outside one last time before bedtime.

ALTERNATING SOLUTIONS

The Anti-Stress Tisane on page 27 can be used alternately with the mixture of lemon balm, passionflower, and valerian in cases when the sleeping problem persists and when the mixture is administered for more than twenty days, which can cause it to lose its effectiveness as the body adapts to it. This is because the liver becomes increasingly effective at eliminating a substance. Alternating the use of different calming solutions helps maintain their potency.

Sexual Excitement

Nowadays, sterilization (both spaying and neutering) has become the most common surgical procedure performed by veterinarians. However, there are still many dogs that remain unsterilized. The behavior of an unsterilized male dog around a female dog in heat can be highly problematic: They may howl day and night, no longer eat, or stop grooming themselves. The most serious consequence is that they may run away, causing unpredictable consequences.

What to Know

Sometimes a dog's age or its state of health does not permit sterilization. Although plant-based solutions do not have the same result as surgical or chemical sterilization, they can offer some help to curb a dog's mating instinct.

Natural Solutions

▶ Two plants well known for their anaphrodisiac properties are hops, which contain a molecule that imitates estrogen and therefore reduces impulses related to the male hormone testosterone while also offering a calming effect, and the chaste tree, or *Vitex agnus-castus* ("chaste lamb"), whose seeds were once chewed by young monks when entering a monastery to calm urges during their solitary conditions. Modern science has found that the chaste tree has sedative and anaphrodisiac qualities.

Chaste Tree Berries

1 to 2 dried chaste tree berries per day for a 22-pound (10 kg) dog

The flavor is very aromatic, so it's best to combine it with a food your dog loves to encourage swallowing it quickly.

Tip: Hops and chaste tree berries can be made as a liquid extract without alcohol. You can also give chaste tree berries to your dog to chew. If they are fresh from the tree, you can double the quantity.

Motion Sickness

Motion sickness, or car sickness, in dogs is a very common and very difficult problem that is not always easy to resolve. Pharmaceutical options are available, but natural remedies can offer relief.

What to Know

Avoid giving your dog any liquids before getting into the car.

Natural Solutions

▶ The most effective solution is ginger, which is available in capsules (1 capsule for a dog weighing 22 to 44 pounds [10 to 20 kg]), but its maximum

WHERE THERE'S A WILL . . .

If you have a dog so prone to car sickness that it avoids the car entirely, try these tips to make it more comfortable. Open the car doors with the engine off and allow the dog to sit there for a while, then offer it a treat. Soon after, repeat these steps, but this time with the engine on. Next, try very short trips with the windows slightly open, then again with them closed. It's best to plan the first trips to destinations that are a positive experience for the dog, such as going to a park for time outdoors, or to visit with a person the dog enjoys.

potency is through administering a few drops of fresh ginger juice an hour before departure and then again just before departure. You can combine the ginger with a liquid mixture of passionflower concentrate, valerian, and lemon balm, which provides a calming effect.

Fresh Ginger Juice

WELLNESS
RECIPE
for DOGS

A small quantity of peeled fresh ginger

1. Crush the ginger using a mortar and pestle and collect the juice with a feeding syringe.

2. Administer 1 drop per 4½ pounds (2 kg) of body weight.

Tip: It's best to avoid giving your dog food or water after intake if the animal is prone to car sickness.

CHAPTER 3

Injuries, Pain, and Illness

Injuries and Wounds

Antibiotics, whose use is best minimized, will always have a place in the care for your pet because they can save lives and help avoid many other complications. This is the case with dog bites, as a dog's mouth contains many bacteria, some of which can be harmful if transmitted.

What to Know

If a dog is bitten by another dog, it is important to use an antibacterial bandage. Natural remedies can help cleanse the wound, improve healing, and even help avoid unwanted licking that could worsen the injury.

Natural Solutions

Topical plant-based preparations can be an ally in the care of a dog bite.

▶ To clean the wound, the Thyme and Rosemary Tisane on page 41 can be used.

▶ A tisane of lavender flowers or lavender hydrosol will also help with healing.

HEALING BY LICKING: A MISCONCEPTION

Contrary to the popular belief that a dog's saliva has healing powers, many veterinarians consider licking to undermine, not help with, healing and hygiene.

▶ Aloe vera gel is soothing and healing for a dog's skin.

▶ Preparing a solution with essential oils diluted in a dispersant and water can also be helpful. Using appropriately diluted essential oil in a spray helps avoid overdosing.

WELLNESS
RECIPE
for DOGS

Thyme *and* Rosemary Tisane

3 tablespoons + 1 teaspoon (50 ml) water

1 tablespoon dried thyme leaves

1 tablespoon dried rosemary leaves

1. Bring the water to a boil and pour it over the leaves. Cover, and let infuse for 5 minutes.

2. Strain it and let it cool.

3. Apply the tisane with a sterile compress.

Important: Always consult a veterinarian when it comes to a wound! Sometimes a surgical procedure may be needed.

Cough

Coughing can be a problem that is both frequent and stubborn in dogs. There is a particular cough called "kennel cough" that is transmitted from one dog to another. Coughing is caused by several bacteria, including *Bordetella bronchiseptica*, as well as viruses, and is extremely contagious.

What to Know

Dogs may contract a cough merely by coming in contact with a sick dog or with nasal secretions from a sick dog. A hoarse, powerful cough is often accompanied by runny eyes and nose, transparent diarrhea and vomiting, or white foaming mucus. A veterinary visit will be necessary to determine the best treatment, which might include some form of antibiotics.

Natural Solutions

When it comes to kennel cough, natural solutions are a great supplement to conventional treatments. With its disinfectant and anti-inflammatory properties, propolis will offer comfort and accelerate recovery. It has a strong flavor, so you may need to mix it with a treat to get your dog to eat it.

▶ Essential oils prepared for inhalation can be effective.

▶ Cleaning the eyes and nose with physiological saline or using the Chamomile Tisane for the Eyes (page 7) can offer relief.

▶ Passionflower (*Passiflora incarnata*), which was used by Indigenous people for its cough-fighting properties, can also be used.

▶ Black radish is particularly recommended because it is an antitussive and loosens bronchial secretions. It can be offered in fresh slices, but dogs do not always appreciate its flavor. Black radish juice is easier to administer. There are also alcohol-free extracts.

Black Radish Juice

Black Radish juice (found in organic food stores)

1. Administer 2–4 drops of juice per 2 ¼ pounds (1 kg) of body weight.

2. It is counterproductive to increase the quantity per dosage because the juice will be most effective in small doses several times a day. This rule applies to all natural solutions.

Tip: Black radish liquid extract can also be used to offer some relief to cardiac cough, which is more serious and requires a veterinarian's attention. This cough is often described as one similar to when a dog is attempting to eliminate something stuck in its throat.

Constipation

Constipation is less common in canines than in felines, but if it occurs, natural solutions can be an effective way to combat it.

What to Know

To maintain regularity, gut flora must be in balance. Probiotics, prebiotics, and spirulina contribute to the good health of the microbiota in the gut. And, as always, be sure to pay attention to the amount of water a dog drinks as well as to the quantity and quality of its food. Plenty of fresh water and the right amount of healthy food positively affect the regularity of both dogs and humans.

Natural Solutions

▶ Orally safe aloe vera gel helps with regularity and contains many bowel-regulating

USE A STABILIZED ORALLY SAFE ALOE VERA GEL

Stabilized orally safe aloe vera gel is suitable for animals. You can measure and freeze doses in an ice cube tray to thaw and use only the amount needed.

polysaccharides, such as acemannan.

▶ The quantity of orally safe aloe vera gel to offer for constipation varies from one dog to another. Start with about 4 drops (0.2 ml) of aloe vera gel per 2¼ pounds (1 kg) of body weight twice a day and increase until you find the most effective dose. In some dogs, it takes about

¼ to ⅜ teaspoon (1 to 2 ml) per 2¼ pounds (1 kg). Most dogs can tolerate this treatment. If a dog is intolerant to it, mild vomiting could occur just after taking it.

▶ Psyllium, the main ingredient in many over-the-counter laxatives for humans, is also available for dogs. Combine psyllium with orally safe aloe vera gel to make it easier to ingest.

Artichoke Juice

1 artichoke

1. Use a juicer for a whole artichoke, or a mortar and pestle to juice just the heart. (Artichoke juice is also commercially available.)

2. Start with a very small dose, 1 drop (0.05 ml) per 2¼ pounds (1 kg), and increase the dosage as needed.

Tips:

▶ The artichoke is a remarkable plant for treating constipation. It is especially effective in older dogs or those with a weak liver.

▶ Aloe vera gel also limits gas production. It is effective in these cases when combined with activated charcoal.

Diarrhea

There are two common causes for diarrhea in dogs: First, dogs typically love to eat what they shouldn't as soon as they are outside. Second, their gut flora is highly sensitive to rapid changes. It takes about three weeks for "good gut bacteria" to adjust to a new diet.

What to Know

Rules to respect during occurrences of diarrhea:

▶ For a puppy, a veterinary visit is essential.

▶ For a young healthy dog, offer only water for twelve hours, then offer an antispasmodic tisane.

▶ For an older dog, consult a veterinarian if you have any concerns.

WHILE WALKING

When on a walk with your dog, take water with you so that your dog does not drink from stagnant water sources. As soon as a dog becomes active, its body needs water, and dogs tend not to worry about the quality of the water they drink!

▶ For a dog that has bloody diarrhea, a veterinary visit is essential

After a fasting period, feeding should resume gradually. Offer the usual food but give smaller quantities for two to three days.

Natural Solutions

Through its healing properties, aloe vera can help with regularity.

▶ Antispasmodic plants, such as linden flowers and spearmint leaves, are very suitable.

▶ Bentonite and montmorillonite clay, prebiotics, probiotics, and activated charcoal (which absorbs toxic gases and molecules) are effective.

▶ For a dog that has chronic diarrhea or inflammatory bowel disease, a veterinary visit is essential.

Diarrhea Solution

WELLNESS RECIPE for DOGS

1 capsule activated charcoal (found at veterinarian clinics, health food stores, or pharmacies)

1 capsule probiotic (found at veterinarian clinics, health food stores, or pharmacies)

For a dog weighing 22 pounds (10 kg), administer 1 or 2 times

a day for 4 to 10 days. Smaller doses for smaller dogs.

Tip: Do not forget about the importance of deworming to help fight cases of diarrhea (see page 21).

Vomiting

Vomiting is a common occurrence in dogs and usually consists of partially digested food. However, when vomit contains a yellow foam (indicating the presence of bile) or if there is any blood present, this may be a cause for concern and may require an emergency veterinary visit.

What to Know

Administering turmeric and ginger juice will help the body eliminate a stomach bacterium called *Helicobacter*.

Natural Solutions

▶ For a single occurrence of vomiting resulting from eating something bad, it should take only a few hours for a dog's system to return to normal. Do not offer food during this time, only water.

▶ For vomiting related to motion sickness, see page 36. In cases of chronic vomiting, natural solutions can be good alternatives to consider compared to the powerful antiemetic drugs now available.

▶ When chronic vomiting is related to stomach irritation (gastritis) aloe vera gel is a recommended natural treatment.

▶ Ginger also has antiemetic and anti-nausea properties (see page 49).

A NATURAL STOMACH CLOCK

Getting to know your dog will help you know when something is an emergency. While you should take vomiting seriously, for some dogs, vomiting a yellow foam can occur when a mealtime is missed. The stomach produces acids that are used for digestion during the meal. If a dog's food bowl does not arrive on time, the stomach undergoes a kind of automatic emptying. This is common among young healthy dogs who may vomit only in this circumstance, so it should not be of concern, but always respect a dog's feeding schedule to avoid this.

Nausea Remedy

Organic ground ginger powder (available at health food stores)

Organic ground turmeric powder (available at health food stores)

Combine the powder and dose according to weight.

If your dog is new to this remedy or sensitive, start with a small dose:

Administer no more than 5 servings per day no matter the weight of the dog—even for a large dog.

Variation: Mix with a safe vegetable oil to administer or mix in your dog's food.

1–10 pounds (up to 4.5 kg)	up to ⅛ tsp (1 gr)
11–20 pounds (4.5 to 9 kg)	⅛ to ¼ tsp (1–2 gr)
21–50 pounds (9 to 23 kg)	1 tsp (4 gr)
51–100 pounds (23 to 45 kg)	2 tsp (8 gr)
Over 100 lbs (45 kg)	1 tbsp (14 gr)

Gut Flora

We often turn to prebiotics and probiotics only when attempting to resolve intestinal problems such as acute diarrhea. This is unfortunate! They hold benefits for balancing gut flora—which is important for overall gut health to fight constipation, improve general immunity, increase nutrient absorption, and even improve mental well-being.

What to Know

When should you offer prebiotics and probiotics to your dog?

It is not necessary to administer prebiotics and probiotics to your dog on an ongoing basis. Instead, opt to do so only when a change creates a need to keep gut flora in check, such as:

▶ when changing the diet, and ideally before the change is made

▶ in cases of increased physical activity (vacation or competitions)

▶ during a major shedding period

▶ during pregnancy (gestation or nursing)

▶ during growth (for large dogs in particular)

▶ during periods of convalescence

▶ during episodes of diarrhea or vomiting

▶ when skin problems occur

▶ in older dogs

▶ to help the flora of other mucous membranes (ears, vagina)

▶ in cases of cystitis

Natural Solutions

▶ Prebiotics are food substances (polysaccharides, also known as sugars) that nourish probiotics (bacteria that promote proper digestive function).

▶ Inulin is a prebiotic substance present in chicory and dandelion root (especially during autumn). It has positive effects on gut flora. This is also the case with aloe vera gel.

▶ Brewer's yeast is now considered a probiotic and is a source of vitamin B, essential for the proper functioning of the nervous system and muscles. At a time when veterinary medicine is increasingly based on scientific evidence, brewer's yeast remains relevant as a method for balancing flora; this in turn has a general positive effect on the health and well-being of our canine companions.

Brewer's Yeast *and* Inulin

WELLNESS
RECIPE
for DOGS

Brewer's yeast

Inulin

1. Administer brewer's yeast as indicated for seasonal shedding on page 3.

2. Administer a small amount of inulin powder—between 50 and 100 mg—in aloe vera gel or sprinkle over your dog's food once a day.

Inflammation

Inflammation is present any time a cell, a group of cells, or an organ malfunctions. Once inflammation occurs, it creates a vicious cycle by aggravating the initial problem. In such cases, plants and natural solutions can help limit inflammation's negative impacts.

Natural Solutions

Natural anti-inflammatories

▶ Phycocyanin, present in spirulina, is well studied for its antioxidant and anti-inflammatory properties. It is good for older dogs or dogs that have a liver, kidney, or pancreas that is not functioning properly. When a dog has problems with cystitis or urine crystals, phycocyanin is recommended rather than spirulina, which is very high in mineral content. Omega-3 fatty acids are also effective.

GINGER: A WEAPON AGAINST INFLAMMATION

Considered one of the healthiest spices in nature, ginger has been used for thousands of years in both traditional and alternative medicinal remedies. It contains several bioactive compounds, called gingerols, that act as a weapon against inflammation. Among its many health benefits, ginger is touted for its ability to relieve joint pain and stiffness by reducing oxidative stress caused by excess inflammation in the body. Ginger can be used in various forms: ground, fresh, or juiced.

▶ Turmeric and its active compound, curcumin, are also good options

▶ Quercetin, a yellow plant pigment, fights inflammation.

Anti-inflammation Paste

WELLNESS **RECIPE** *for DOGS*

1 teaspoon turmeric powder per 11 pounds (5 kg) of body weight

1 teaspoon olive oil per 11 pounds (5 kg) of body weight

1. Combine the ingredients.

2. Mix the paste in your dog's food or administer it directly.

Tip: Combining the ground turmeric with a vegetable oil or olive oil improves the bioavailability of turmeric. Note that although black pepper and turmeric are a powerfully healthy combination for humans, black pepper can irritate a dog's system and should be avoided.

Joint and Muscle Pain

When it comes to treating joint and muscle pain with natural cures, first determine if the pain is short-term and severe or short-term and mild.

What to Know

▶ Acute, severe pain can be caused by an accident, injury, or fall. When this happens, we must act fast to treat it. A veterinary visit will determine the severity and recommended treatment. Natural remedies can be offered along with any recommended treatments and can continue to be administered alone over extended periods once pain starts to subside.

▶ Short-term mild pain can occur in cases such as a puppy falling out of bed or bumping into a piece of furniture while playing. It can also be aches and pains experienced after a long session of play between dogs or from a long walk. In these milder cases, you can start by offering a natural remedy. However, if after twenty-four hours the pain does not appear to improve, a veterinary visit will determine if stronger treatment is necessary.

Natural Solutions

▶ Turmeric has a long history of use in Ayurvedic medicine to treat pain, and its properties are now appreciated more widely in Western medicine.

▶ Boswellia, another plant used in Ayurvedic medicine, is a valuable ally against pain due to its compounds, boswellic acids, which are antinociceptive, meaning they inhibit the brain's perception of pain. Studies have shown that Boswellia can be an effective painkiller due to its anti-inflammatory properties.

▶ Other plants, such as meadowsweet and black currant, can be very useful. Black currant bud exists in an alcohol-free form that is well suited to dogs.

Turmeric *and* Boswellia Paste

RECIPE
WELLNESS
for DOGS

1 pinch teaspoon ground turmeric per 11 pounds (5 kg) of body weight

1 pinch teaspoon ground Boswellia per 11 pounds (5 kg) of body weight

Combine the ingredients, then add a few drops of water to make a bright orange paste, which can be applied directly on the dog's tongue.

Variation: If you have capsules, you can administer 1 capsule of turmeric and 1 capsule of Boswellia for a dog weighing 22 pounds (10 kg). Half a capsule for dogs 10–20 pounds (5 kg), a quarter capsule for smaller dogs.

Tip: An over-the-counter, prepared solution can be more convenient, especially if it is flavored in a way to suit the dog.

Early Age–Related Pain

Dogs are energetic animals and love to walk. They experience little joint discomfort in their early years, but as soon as you observe them getting up with a little difficulty or a certain amount of stiffness, you should consider ways to bring them comfort.

What to Know

Starting from age seven in small- or medium-sized dogs and from age three in some very large breeds, it is a good idea to start offering your pet solutions that help delay the breakdown of cartilage that protects the joints. Once cartilage is gone, it does not regenerate. Consider treatment on an occasional basis first, then on a more permanent basis as the dog ages.

Natural Solutions

▶ Food supplements known as "chondroprotectors" (cartilage protectors) are often sufficient at the very beginning of a dog's growth period. These supplements help limit inflammation and provide comfort to a dog experiencing joint pain when it gets up or participates in an activity. Chondroprotectors include glucosamine sulfate, chondroitin sulfate, type II collagen, turmeric, and Boswellia.

▶ For preventative measures, offer spirulina or chondroprotectors.

▶ When mild discomfort sets in, alternate between nettle extract, silica, black currant bud extract, turmeric, meadowsweet, Boswellia, or quercetin.

▶ If you have not been offering preventative measures, start with chondroprotective cures during autumn and winter months. If discomfort is present but mild, consider a treatment of nettle and silica, as well as spirulina for an extended period.

When returning from a long walk or when the weather is cold and wet, add turmeric and Boswellia. If your dog is already taking a chondroprotector, alternate it with plant-based remedies (turmeric, Boswellia, nettle).

Nettle Paste

WELLNESS
RECIPE
for DOGS

1 capsule nettle tops for a 22-pound (10 kg) dog. Divide accordingly for smaller dogs.

Open the capsule and add a few drops of water at a time to the contents to make a paste that you can spread on your dog's mouth.

Variation: Alternatively, mix the nettle tops with your dog's favorite dish to minimize the smell and taste or administer them in a feeding syringe with about ¼ teaspoon (1 ml) of water.

Tip: Use this remedy during the autumn and winter months.

Age-Related Pain

Although we may prefer to fight a dog's pain without the use of conventional drugs, certain cases of pain make them necessary. But natural remedies can still play a role to help provide comfort to suffering pets.

Natural Solutions

▶ Combining natural solutions with conventional treatment to assist with improved mobility can reduce the amount of traditional medication needed. Turmeric and Boswellia are good options (see page 55).

▶ Natural anti-inflammation solutions are a good supplement for dogs undergoing traditional pharmaceutical treatment for pain (see page 53). In addition, natural solutions, such as turmeric and spirulina, help protect the liver, kidney, and pancreas from the potential negative effects of traditional pain-fighting medication.

A RECOMMENDED PROTOCOL FOR PAIN

Always follow your vet's care instructions, but generally, administer conventional treatment for one to four days as soon as pain is observed. Begin natural solutions (turmeric, Boswellia, ginger) at the same time and administer them for at least twenty days. Use spirulina for at least twenty days to support the liver and kidneys.

Turmeric *and* Ginger Juice

WELLNESS RECIPE for DOGS

▶ Use a ready-made turmeric ginger juice for freshness.

WEIGHT	DOSE
1–10 pounds (up to 4.5 kg)	1 teaspoon (5 ml)
11–20 pounds (4.5 to 9 kg)	2 teaspoons (10 ml)
21–50 pounds (9 to 23 kg)	3 teaspoons (15 ml)
51 pounds and over (23 kg)	1 tablespoon (30 ml)

Tip: As always, start with a low dose to see how your dog tolerates it. Feel free to freeze individual portions in an ice cube tray for up to two months.

The Liver

The liver is a vital organ essential to a dog's good health. It acts as a sort of "manufacturing plant" of many substances essential to life, as well as acts as the main "waste reprocessing plant" by removing toxins from the body. If the liver is not functioning properly, your companion can experience a wide variety of complications.

What to Know

The liver processes nutrients from digested food. It also breaks down toxins and helps eliminate them. It plays a major role in the manufacture of blood and in matters related to immunity and inflammation. The liver also produces bile, which aids with digestion, and it is the only organ that can regenerate itself. Despite its importance, however, it is often neglected.

Natural Solutions

▶ Spirulina, red fruit anthocyanins, milk thistle, turmeric, artichoke, dandelion, and black radish are natural liver-friendly solutions.

KEYS TO A HEALTHY LIVER

Good liver health requires low inflammation and protected liver cells that function well. A healthy diet, good hydration, and sufficient blood supply (promoted by regular physical activity) are keys to a healthy liver.

▶ Desmodium, also known as tick clover, is an African plant often used to fight jaundice. It protects the liver and gallbladder.

Liver Support Remedy

WELLNESS RECIPE for DOGS

Bottle of desmodium

Bottle of black currant juice— available at natural food stores

1. Combine an equal amount of both juices.

2. Administer 2–4 times a day.

WEIGHT	DOSE
2–10 pounds (1–4.5 kg)	½ to 1 teaspoon (2–5 ml)
11–20 pounds (4.5–9 kg)	1–2 teaspoons (5–10 ml)
21–50 pounds (9–23 kg)	2–3 teaspoons (10–15 ml)
51 pounds and over (23 kg)	3–4 teaspoons (15–30 ml)

The Kidneys

The kidneys are small, vital organs that perform two major functions: purifying the blood and secreting hormones. The hormones regulate blood pressure and produce red blood cells. The kidneys also regulate the amount of water in all organs and eliminate waste and toxic substances.

What to Know

The first signs of weakened kidneys are an increase in the amount of water a dog drinks as well as occasional vomiting. These signs are subtle, so the only way to know if your dog has kidney problems is to have a veterinarian take blood tests.

In case of kidney problems, it is necessary to:

▶ reduce inflammation (see page 52)

▶ protect cells (phycocyanin, black currant; see pages 31/61)

▶ help with waste disposal (a diuretic tisane; see page 63)

PRECAUTIONS

Always provide access to fresh water and take your dog out regularly.

Natural Solutions

▶ Dandelion, *Orthosiphon stamineus*, orange hawkweed, linden, boldo, and black currant

are plants that help with the elimination of waste.

Diuretic Tisane

3 tablespoons + 1 teaspoon (50 ml) water

1 tablespoon dried orthosiphon leaves

1 tablespoon boldo leaves

1. Bring the water to a boil and pour it over the leaves. Cover, and let infuse for 5 minutes.

2. Strain it and let it cool.

3. Administer about 2 drops (0.1 ml) per 2¼ pounds (1 kg) of body weight 2 to 4 times a day.

The Bladder

Cystitis is inflammation of the bladder and is very painful. The disease affects female dogs more often than male dogs. If this condition occurs, always see a veterinarian and treat the condition aggressively.

What to Know

For cystitis, antibiotics and conventional painkillers should be considered. In the case of chronic cystitis that occurs in some dogs, natural remedies can be of great help. If urine crystals and infection are no longer present, natural preparations are a good choice to help prevent inflammation (see page 52), avoid a future crisis, and help balance gut flora (see page 50). The quality and quantity of water a dog drinks daily should be monitored closely.

Natural Solutions

▶ Blueberry anthocyanins—the most healing part of the blueberry in an extracted form—are an effective solution for bladder issues. Cranberry is a popular treatment but taking cranberry over long periods of time can "acidify the body," which simply means having too much acid in the body, making your pet very uncomfortable. Blueberry anthocyanins avoid this.

Blueberry Juice

WELLNESS
RECIPE
for DOGS

Bottled blueberry juice,
available in health food
stores (no sugar added!)

1. Administer 2 drops (0.1 ml)
per 2¼ pounds (1 kg) of body
weight.

2. Offer two times a day
for 2–4 months. Always
follow up with your vet.

Alternative: You can make your
own juice by mashing blueberries
or using a juicer.

Precaution: If your vet is
concerned about cystitis or urine
crystals, do not give your dog
spirulina, as it is rich in minerals,
which is undesirable in these
cases.

The Heart

Dogs often develop heart problems as they age. Veterinary medicine has evolved considerably in the treatment of heart problems, in terms of both diagnosis and available medications. Combining traditional treatment with natural solutions offers a comfortable life to a dog with these problems, which is a great victory over the condition.

What to Know

To safeguard your dog's heart, you need to:

▶ support the liver when taking medication (see page 60)

▶ increase urination (see Diuretic Tisane, page 63)

▶ fight against cough (see page 42)

Natural Solutions

There are plants suitable for supporting the heart that we might be tempted to use instead of traditional medicines, but in cases of heart problems it's best to choose conventional treatment while providing support to the organs as indicated above.

▶ Plants friendly to dogs with heart problems are dandelion, black currant (slightly diuretic and anti-inflammatory), *Orthosiphon stamineus*, orange hawkweed, and passionflower.

▶ Spirulina is a good choice in cases of heart problems.

A SOOTHING MASSAGE

When a cardiac cough is very strong, a dog may panic, which causes a vicious cycle leading to even more coughing. If this happens, open a window and sit next to your dog (the dog is often better sitting than standing). Using your hand, massage your dog starting from the chin to the bottom of the neck. At the same time, talk to your dog calmly and breathe slowly so that the dog matches your breathing rate.

Soothing Massage Gel

WELLNESS
RECIPE
for DOGS

2 tablespoons aloe vera gel

1 teaspoon xanthan gum powder

2 tablespoons orange blossom hydrosol

1. Thoroughly combine all the ingredients.

2. Use as needed.

3. Store in the refrigerator for up to 7 days.

The Brain

Dogs are living longer and longer and, like us, sometimes become disoriented in their old age, becoming confused about their surroundings and developing habits that can make them forget cleanliness, their day-night routine, etc. This can be accompanied by changes in mood, barking and restlessness, or even despondency, sadness, and depression. Some dogs may want to lie down all day or refuse to eat.

What to Know

When it comes to taking care of your dog's brain, it is essential to maintain a good quality of life, regular physical activity, a rich canine social life, and to:

▶ fight inflammation (see page 52)

▶ assist with adaptation (see page 28)

▶ limit disorientation (see page 69)

▶ promote sleep (see page 33)

▶ fight stress (see page 26)

Natural Solutions

▶ For brain health, we must consider the dog's overall health because an aging brain will have repercussions to the whole body. Plant-based remedies are a good option as they contain many substances that act upon different levels of the body.

▶ Fish oil, spinach, blueberries, sweet potatoes, and coconut oil are all good foods for your dog's brain.

Brain Health Treats

WELLNESS
RECIPE
for DOGS

Coconut oil

Almond butter

Blueberries

1. Melt a few teaspoons of coconut oil and coat the bottom of each small mold in a silicone tray.

2. Add about a teaspoon of almond butter to each mold and top with a blueberry.

3. Fill remainder of each mold with coconut oil.

4. Freeze for 15–20 minutes.

5. Give your dog a few treats a day, depending on her weight and eating habits.

The Skin

The skin is the body's largest organ. Its role as both a barrier and a zone of exchange with the external environment exposes it to many potential problems, so when considering a dog's skin health, we must think in terms of its body as a whole.

What to Know

In dogs, skin problems are common. Pruritus, or itching, negatively impacts the lives of many dogs, and consequently their families, as a dog that itches and scratches is a dog that lives in discomfort.

Natural Solutions

▶ A dog that suffers from skin problems must have its health

A VETERINARIAN'S TALE

As a veterinarian, I've seen many dogs with skin problems, such as was the case with Maya, an adorable chow who was just two years old when I met her. She was being treated for itching and had serious joint problems and seemed depressed. I felt especially that Maya also seemed bored. What touched me most, however, was seeing the commitment of her family, who looked for any remedy that could help. I discussed natural treatment with them and advised them on solutions I believed would help. When I saw Maya again at age five, she was transformed. She was no longer taking medication, and her itching and scratching were gone. Her family said she now spends two hours a day walking in a large, wooded park nearby where the family had moved from the city to a house in the suburbs.

addressed comprehensively by:

- ▶ balancing gut flora (see page 50)
- ▶ fighting inflammation (see page 52)
- ▶ protecting the liver (see page 60)
- ▶ fighting stress (see page 26)

- ▶ Rose hydrosol is cleansing and regenerating.
- ▶ Marshmallow powder is calming, softening, and emollient, and its mucilage helps moisturize the skin.
- ▶ Colloidal oats are calming and conditioning.
- ▶ Aloe vera gel is calming, healing, and renewing.

Soothing Skin Gel

WELLNESS
RECIPE
for DOGS

About ¼ teaspoon colloidal oats

1 teaspoon marshmallow powder

1 tablespoon rose hydrosol

1 tablespoon aloe vera gel

1 teaspoon xanthan gum powder

1. Combine all the ingredients and mix well.

2. Apply to the irritated part of your dog's skin.

Tip: Fresh fig juice, best when figs are picked from the tree just before application, eliminates warts. The juice should be applied only to the wart (as it is caustic to the skin) several times until it disappears.

The Pancreas

The pancreas is a small organ that is usually forgotten about when it functions properly but can cause many problems and suffering when it fails to do so.

What to Know

The pancreas has two functions:

▶ Disseminate pancreatic juices, which are essential for digestion. These are emptied into the intestine.

▶ Secrete insulin, which is emptied into the bloodstream and regulates blood sugar levels. During acute pancreatitis (inflammation of the pancreas) the pain can be terrible, and the problems with the digestive system (vomiting and diarrhea) must be treated urgently, often requiring hospitalization to help with a cure. During cases of chronic pancreatitis, symptoms are less severe, and natural remedies can offer help.

Natural Solutions

▶ Natural remedies do not target the pancreas specifically, but they can help improve the quality of life for a dog who suffers from pancreatitis. They make it possible to:

> ▶ fight inflammation (see page 52)

> ▶ help balance gut flora (see page 50)

▶ The combination of aloe vera gel, phycocyanin, and blueberry anthocyanins can offer comfort.

▶ Lack of appetite is a major problem in dogs with pancreatitis. Gentian root is very bitter, and the bitter taste helps stimulate appetite.

Pancreas Support

WELLNESS
RECIPE
for DOGS

Gentian root extract free of sugar or alcohol

Administer 2–4 drops (.1 to .5 ml) once a day.

Tip: Gentian root extract is available in health food stores.

Cancer

According to some statistics, one in two dogs over the age of ten are at risk of developing cancer.

What to Know

Conventional treatments for animal cancers have progressed considerably in the last few years, making a diagnosis not as scary as it once was. Many dogs recover, and plants and natural solutions have their place alongside medical treatments. Although natural solutions cannot eradicate cancer, they can bring much comfort and well-being to the canine patient.

Natural Solutions

▶ If your dog develops cancer, find comprehensive management by a veterinarian trained in the use of plants and natural solutions. For essential comprehensive care, the following should be considered:

▶ strengthening gut flora (see page 50)

▶ fighting inflammation (see page 52)

▶ fighting pain (see pages 54–59)

▶ protecting the liver (see page 60)

▶ protecting the kidneys (see page 62)

▶ fighting stress (see page 26)

▶ assisting with adaptation (see page 28)

▶ A combination of phycocyanin and blueberry anthocyanins is a concentrated antioxidant solution that can improve quality of life.

▶ Aloe vera gel regulates digestion. It also helps with healing and supports the immune system. It can be combined with conventional treatments.

▶ Natural aloe in very small doses can be administered once a day every day.

Cancer and Medicinal Mushrooms

Mushrooms are a well-studied topic in cancer treatment due to their antioxidants, which lend them many beneficial properties.

What to Know

Do not offer your dog mushrooms during radiation treatment. The goal of radiation treatment is to destroy a tumor by causing oxidation, and medicinal mushrooms contain molecules (beta-glucans, polysaccharides) with powerful antioxidant properties. Always be aware of a mushroom's origins and avoid those treated with pesticides that may contain heavy metals.

Natural Solutions

▶ Offer a mixture of shiitake, maitake, and reishi mushrooms in combination with phycocyanin and blueberry anthocyanins.

HOW TO FEED MUSHROOMS TO YOUR DOG

You can offer your dog fresh mushrooms, but it can be difficult to calculate the dosage correctly in this way. It is more accurate and easier to administer tablets (on average, a dosage would be 1 tablet for a 22-pound [10 kg] dog). For a very small dog, you may need to crush the tablet and offer just a small amount mixed with a little water or oil to facilitate intake.

Medicinal Mushroom Solution

Medicinal mushroom capsule

1. Open the capsule and empty the contents into a small bowl.

2. Mix with a small amount of water.

3. Give your dog the contents of one capsule for 22 pounds (10 kg) of body weight, once a day.

Tip: As always, start with a small amount to see how your dog tolerates it.

Plants and Surgery

When our beloved canine companions must undergo surgery, it can cause a great deal of anxiety for all those involved. Natural solutions can be beneficial before and after a surgical procedure.

What to Know

Avoid administering natural solutions to your dog the day before and the day of the surgery to avoid interfering with the medicines used during the procedure.

Natural Solutions

What are beneficial natural solutions before and after surgery?

▶ Spirulina facilitates healing.

▶ Turmeric is an antioxidant and protects the liver and kidney cells.

PRECAUTIONS

Ginkgo biloba thins the blood, so stop administering it four days before your dog undergoes an operation. This also applies to natural remedies using willow or meadowsweet.

▶ Aloe vera helps with healing.

▶ Plants offer soothing properties and fight stress (see page 26).

Pre-Surgery Support

Blueberry juice

1. Beginning ten days before surgery, offer your dog 2 drops (.1 ml) per 2¼ pounds (1 kg) of body weight.

2. Do not give your dog the juice the day before or the day of the surgery.

3. Resume offering the juice two days after surgery and continue for 20 days.

Tip: Spirulina for liver support and ginger to reduce nausea are also helpful.

Plants and Pregnancy

There are holistic preparations that have been used for generations that offer support during pregnancy for all species, including dogs that are postnatal.

What to Know

The periods of pregnancy, birth, and nursing are perfect times to offer natural solutions for the mother in order to avoid exposing the puppies to chemical substances through the placenta or mother's milk.

Natural Solutions

▶ When puppies nurse, they cause small irritations of the mother's teats, which can cause discomfort. Applying a cleansing and healing solution that is also safe for the puppies, such as one composed of a thyme tisane and aloe vera gel, is a good option.

Cleansing *and* Healing Tisane

**3 tablespoons + 1 teaspoon (50 ml)
water**

1 teaspoon thyme leaves

1 tablespoon aloe vera gel

1. Bring the water to a boil and pour it over the leaves. Cover, and let infuse for 5 minutes.

2. Strain it and let it cool.

3. Combine it with the aloe vera gel. Apply by gently dabbing with a compress on irritated areas.

Tip: At the time of nursing, when the mother has swollen teats and the puppies are not feeding, fresh parsley is a useful solution to decrease milk flow. Finely chop 1 tablespoon of parsley for a dog weighing 22 pounds (10 kg) and administer 1 or 2 times a day.

Your Natural Dog

Plants offer numerous opportunities to assist with dogs' well-being, but it can be difficult to explore them all. With access to the internet, we can now more easily find information and products needed to achieve customized natural solutions for our dogs. The best advice, however, is to not overcomplicate the process.

To best preserve your homemade natural remedies, do not

store large quantities of them. Buy what you need in small quantities and make only what is needed for a single application.

With just a little organization and care and attention to your dog's reactions to the natural remedies offered, you can quickly realize positive results that you will be encouraged to repeat. Trust yourself and be creative. By doing this, you can create benefits for the dog you love—and who loves you!

Aways consult your supportive veterinarian before beginning or administering any natural cure.

About the Author

Céline Gastinel-Moussour is a veterinary doctor, licensed since 1994. Passionate about animals and plants her entire life, she established a phytotherapy consultation practice in 2003 and honed her skills with a university degree at Clermont-Ferrand in 2006 while maintaining her practice as a general veterinarian open to natural solutions.

Driven by her desire to learn and teach, she published her first book in 2009, followed by several others in 2011, 2013, and 2015. She shares her knowledge with all those who want it, especially veterinarians and veterinary students, more and more of whom are interested in plants that are beneficial to animals.

Index of Ingredients